CONTENTS

A NUN LIKE NO OTHER

On 5th September 1997, an 87-year-old nun died in Kolkata, in India.

Normally an old lady passing away wouldn't make even the local news, but this story spread across the globe immediately. Why? The old lady was Mother Teresa – a nun like no other.

RELUCTANTLY FAMOUS

By the time she died, Mother Teresa was one of the most famous people in the world; known for the work she did helping the poor and dying, particularly in Kolkata. However, she was never happy being in the limelight – in fact, she only tolerated the attention because it also raised money for her work. It was partly this unwillingness to be a celebrity that made her so popular with people.

▶ Mother Teresa always wore a simple white tunic called a habit, with blue stripes around the edge.

▲ The Howrah flower market in Kolkata is busy, bright and colourful. Local people use the flowers to make offerings to their Hindu gods.

UNEXPECTED JOURNEY

Mother Teresa was the head of an order of nuns with convents all around the world. The order's headquarters were in Kolkata: this is where Mother Teresa called home, and she became famous for living there. This was not always the case, though. Mother Teresa herself was not Indian and her life began on a very different course, and in a very different place, to where it ended. So how did this quiet, unassuming nun become so famous – and what was it exactly that she did? It is an amazing story…

IN THE BEGINNING

Name: Anjezë Gonxha Bojaxhiu

Born: Skopje, Macedonia

Date of Birth: 26 August 1910

Died: Kolkata, India

Date of Death: 5 September 1997

Parents: Nikollë Bojaxhiu (father), Dranafile Bernai (mother)

Brother: Lazar

Sister: Aga (sometimes written as Age)

Languages spoken: Albanian, Serbo-Croat, Latin, English, Bengali and Hindi

Religion: Roman Catholic

Interests: Poetry, singing and playing the mandolin

The baby who would grow up to be Mother Teresa was born in Skopje, a city in what is now Macedonia, in 1910.

She was baptised the day after she was born, and named Anjezë Gonxha Bojaxhiu. The name 'Gonxha' is Albanian for 'flower bud' and this, rather than Anjezë, was how she was usually known.

▼ Today, Skopje is a bustling modern city with more than half a million inhabitants. It is the capital of Macedonia, in Eastern Europe.

► Gonxha and her sister Aga dressed up in traditional Macedonian costumes, in 1923.

POLITICAL UPHEAVAL

Gonxha's family were ethnic Albanians living in Skopje. She shared her home with her mother, father, brother Lazar, and sister Aga. Gonxha's father, Nikollë, was a successful businessman, so the family were well off. However, these were turbulent times – in the early part of the 20th century, countries were jostling with each other for power and territory. By Gonxha's fourth birthday, Europe had been plunged into World War I. Nikollë became increasingly involved in politics, and the house was often visited by politicians.

▲ Gonxha's father, Nikollë Bojaxhiu, in 1919.

TRAGEDY

Gonxha was unaware of the importance of these meetings, but soon after the war ended, there were terrible consequences for her family. Skopje and the surrounding area was part of Serbia at the time, and Nikollë spoke up for the rights of the Albanians living there. In 1919, he travelled to a political meeting in Belgrade, the Serbian capital. He returned terribly ill and died days later. Many people suspected that he had been deliberately poisoned by political opponents. Overnight, the Bojaxhius lost not just their father, but also his business and along with it the family's income. They were facing ruin.

EARLY INTERESTS

When Nikollë died, Gonxha's mother, Dranafile, was determined that her family would not crumble.

She became a businesswoman herself, selling cloth, embroidery and even carpets so that she could provide for her family. It was a great example to Gonxha about what could be achieved through hard work, and not the only useful lesson that Gonxha learned first-hand from her parents.

OPEN HOUSE

The Bojaxhiu family were very religious. They went to Mass at their local church every morning and put their Christian belief in helping people into practice at home. For as long as Gonxha could remember, there had always been regular guests at her house for meals. The family invited friends, but also people who had fallen on hard times. Helping those less fortunate was a feature of Gonxha's childhood. She often went out with her mother to visit the poor, taking them food, helping around their houses and – perhaps most importantly – showing them they were cared for.

▲ Gonxha on her confirmation day in 1921. Her mother, Dranafile, is on the right of the picture.

▲ Gonxha (3rd from left) photographed in 1920 with her classmates at school.

SCHOOLDAYS

Like most young children, Gonxha also enjoyed playing with her friends and going to school. The first school she attended was attached to her church, the Sacred Heart, but as she got older she went to a state school. In 1921, a Catholic religious order called the Jesuits was responsible for running Gonxha's local church. The priest in charge, Father Gaspar Zadrima, was so impressed with her knowledge and faith that the following year he asked her to help – even though she was only 12 years old. Gonxha taught the younger children their catechism; a series of instructions on what Catholics believe and how they should lead their lives. Also around this time, Gonxha learned of the work of missionaries, and became fascinated by their lives and faith.

Missionaries

A missionary is someone who goes to a foreign country to spread the word of God. Usually missionaries are part of a religious order and also teach, help the poor, or work in hospitals or medical centres.

▲ Father Jambrekovic - the priest that had such
an influence on Gonxha's life - photographed at her school.

In 1924, a new priest called Father Jambrekovic took charge of Gonxha's parish.

He introduced a religious group called a sodality, which Gonxha joined. The sodality mixed social events with religious activities such as questioning what each member was doing to live a full Christian life. As she pondered the answers to questions such as these, Gonxha began to wonder whether God was calling her to do something more.

INSPIRING LETTERS

It was also through Father Jambrekovic that Gonxha got to hear more about the work of missionaries. He used to read out letters that had been sent to him by Jesuit priests working in India.

The letters described their work, and – more excitingly – these missionaries would occasionally visit Skopje and talk about what they had been doing. Previously Gonxha had known of the missions in Africa, but she became inspired by what was happening in India. She had found her calling, and was determined to join them. Gonxha spent a long time thinking and praying about her decision. However, by the time she was eighteen years old she was convinced that it was the right one. There was an order of nuns working in Bengal, in India, called the Sisters of Loreto, and Gonxha resolved to join them.

▲ Before leaving for Ireland, Gonxha (centre) spent time with Aga (left) and friends.

FAMILY TENSIONS

However, just because she was sure of her calling did not mean her family welcomed her decision. In fact, her brother Lazar was very unhappy with her choice. He could not understand why Gonxha wanted to become a nun, and was quite angry about it. Gonxha's mother, too, was upset and initially refused to allow her to do it. Yet Gonxha persisted with her dream. Eventually her mother realised that Gonxha was truly determined, and gave her daughter her blessing.

The Catholic Church

There are more than one billion Catholics in the world today. They are Christians, which means they follow the teachings of Jesus. The head of the Catholic Church is the Pope and Catholics trace their religion back to Saint Peter the apostle (follower of Jesus), who was the first pope.

LIFE AS A NUN

It was no surprise that Gonxha's family greeted her decision to become a nun with mixed reactions.

Becoming a nun meant that Gonxha had to give herself to God; she would not be allowed to get married or have children. Gonxha was to be a missionary, too, which meant she would be sent to work in far-away countries. When she left to study to become a nun, they knew there was a good chance they might never see her again.

▲ Gonxha (to the left of the photograph) in training to be a nun in Darjeeling.

NEW COUNTRY, NEW LANGUAGE

In addition, the order of nuns that Gonxha chose to join had their headquarters thousands of miles from her family home in Skopje. The Sisters of Loreto were based just outside the city of Dublin in Ireland. This was a problem in more ways than one – firstly it was a long way away, and secondly Gonxha didn't speak English! But before she could go to Ireland, she had to have an interview to make sure she was doing the right thing, and that the order was the right place for her. On 26th September 1928, Gonxha boarded a train for Paris, France where the Sisters of Loreto had a hostel and where her interview was to take place.

A NEW NAME

Gonxha passed the interview and made her way to Ireland from Paris, where she spent about six weeks learning English. Then she was on the move again, this time to the order's base in Darjeeling, India. Here she was to learn how to become a nun. It was also time to choose the name by which she would be known for the rest of her life – Teresa, after the saint Thérèse of Lisieux. Gonxha now had a new life and a new name!

◄ Saint Thérèse of Lisieux died at the early age of 24, but has become a hugely popular saint. This statue of her is in Notre Dame Cathedral, in Paris.

What's in a Name?

Nuns change their name as a sign that they have started a new life, although not all nuns do this; it depends on which order they have joined. If a nun chooses to change her name, she often takes the name of a saint that has particularly inspired her. Teresa chose her name because Saint Thérèse is the patron saint of missions. Teresa used the Spanish spelling of the name because another nun in the order had already chosen the name Thérèse.

A CALL WITHIN A CALL

▲ Teresa (top right) taking her vows to become a nun. This signalled the end of her time in Darjeeling.

Teresa had come a long way from Skopje in quite a short space of time, and after her whirlwind of travel, her time in Darjeeling felt quite peaceful.

This didn't mean she had an easy life, though – as well as learning how to be a nun, she also studied the Hindi and Bengali languages she would need in India. In addition, Teresa worked as a teacher, something she had enjoyed doing when teaching catechism back home. After two years, her training was over and Teresa took her final vows – she was now a nun.

ARRIVING IN KOLKATA

It was time to move, too; this time to the order's House, called the Loreto Entally, in the Indian city of Kolkata. After the peace and tranquillity of Darjeeling, the bustling city of Kolkata was a real change – it was busy, noisy and there seemed, to Teresa's eyes, to be poverty everywhere. However Teresa's job was to teach rather than to help the poor. There were two schools in Loreto Entally, one for European girls who boarded there, and the other for Indian girls. Teresa taught in both schools.

MOTHER TERESA

By 1937, at the age of just 26, she was not only the head teacher of both schools, but also Mother Superior and now known as Mother Teresa.

This meant she was in charge of all of the nuns in that particular House. Although she was very happy, something was troubling her. All of her work was inside the compound where the House was based. Yet outside she knew there were so many people in need of help. Every Sunday she went out and visited the poor and suffering. That felt like the right thing to do – after all, it was why she had wanted to become a missionary. Was God calling to her again?

▼ The crowds of homeless people sleeping on the streets of Kolkata shocked Sister Teresa.

Kolkata

Kolkata is in the northeast of India, and is the capital city of the area known as Bengal. It used to be the capital city of the whole of India, before it was replaced by New Delhi in 1911. With more than 4 million residents, Kolkata is India's third largest city.

THE MISSIONARIES OF CHARITY

While Mother Teresa contemplated her future, the world was plunged into chaos again.

In 1939, World War II began in Europe. India was part of the British Empire, and was dragged into the conflict. Loreto Entally was taken over as a hospital for wounded soldiers and the nuns had to move elsewhere in the city. The war coincided with a terrible famine in India – the needs of the poor could not have been greater.

A NEW CALL

After the war was over, there were further problems in Kolkata. In 1946, religious disturbances between the Hindus and Muslims led to riots and killings, and the situation for those living in poverty was becoming increasingly desperate. Mother Teresa was convinced God was calling her to go out on the streets and form a new order to help those in need, and she was determined to do it. She persuaded her local archbishop to allow her to leave her order and set up a new one for a trial period of one year. The conditions were that she had to recruit at least nine trainee nuns (called novices), and that she underwent further medical training.

▶ By 1943, the famine in India was taking a terrible toll. Men, women and children were starving to death.

AN ORDER FROM NOTHING

It was December 1948, and Mother Teresa wasted no time getting things organized. She did her training and wrote to all her ex-students to ask if anyone would like to join her. A wealthy family in Kolkata gave her rooms on the third floor of their house to use as a base. Mother Teresa also designed a new habit for her nuns to wear. It was based on an Indian sari and was made of simple white cloth with the edges trimmed in blue. She also came up with a name for her order – the Missionaries of Charity. Over the next few weeks, novices arrived and a school was set up to teach poor children. Mother Teresa had answered her calling.

▶ As word spread about the work of Mother Teresa and her novices, more and more people wanted to join her order.

Setting up an order

Setting up a new religious order is not straightforward. Only the pope can give permission for a new permanent order, and he only does so when it has been proved that there is a real need for it. Mother Teresa used her trial period as proof that there was a need for the Missionaries of Charity.

SPIRITUAL LIFE AND TEACHINGS

Mother Teresa was used to a simple life. Although her family had been well off when she was young, they had never had a lavish lifestyle.

Nor had her time with the Sisters of Loreto been particularly comfortable. Now that she was in charge of her own order, she was determined to stay true to her principles.

A SIMPLE LIFE

The Missionaries were working with some of the poorest people in the world, and the nuns had to live a life that reflected this. Mother Teresa insisted that each nun had very few possessions: two tunics each (one to wear and one to dry after washing); their saris, underwear and sandals; a metal bucket to wash in; a thin sleeping mat and a crucifix. All the nuns slept in one dormitory and ate simple, plain meals. They woke at 4.40 a.m. and began the day with prayers at 5.00 a.m, followed by Mass.

Between breakfast and lunch they tended to the poor, providing food, basic medical help and anything else they could to lessen their suffering. The afternoon was spent in prayer and meditation followed by tea, then they went back on the streets in the early evening to help the disadvantaged. There were prayers at 9.00 p.m. and then bed at 9.45 p.m.

◀ Mother Teresa bringing comfort to a man in her order's House for the dying.

▲ The simply furnished room that Mother Teresa used in the Mother House in Kolkata. It was here she slept, prayed and worked.

A PLACE OF SAFETY

Mother Teresa's guiding principles were love, dignity and humility. She opened medical centres, and a place where the terminally ill could come to die in a clean and caring environment. Underpinning her work was courage. She often faced threats of violence from people who did not understand or mistrusted her intentions. She met her foes head on, and spoke to them to reassure them of her aims. As a result her House remained a safe place.

Crisis

Although Mother Teresa wrote many letters, articles and books on her work and her faith, she often suffered doubts. At times, she felt as if God was not there or not listening, and she sometimes wondered if she had done the right thing. However she continued her work, having faith that all would be well.

GLOBAL IMPACT

The trial year flew past and it was clear that it was a success. Mother Teresa had shown there was a great need for the Missionaries of Charity.

The archbishop sent a letter of recommendation to Rome suggesting that the order be formally recognized. In 1950, Mother Teresa's prayers were answered, and the Pope approved the request; her order was to be permanent.

OUTCASTS

There was still much to do in Kolkata. Around 2 million destitute people lived in the city – far too many for the authorities and Mother Teresa to deal with, but she always strived to do as much as possible. She moved into a larger property so she could help more people, and persuaded the authorities to set up pumps in the slums so residents had access to clean water.

▼ Mother Teresa handing out Christmas presents of bags of rice and blankets to lepers living in Kolkata in 1971.

Her care even extended to those suffering from leprosy – a terrible disease that meant its sufferers were treated as outcasts; forcing them to live apart from everyone else. The Missionaries visited leper colonies to bring comfort to the sick.

EXPANSION

All the while, the number of novices joining the order grew. In 1960, Mother Teresa decided it was time the order expanded and she opened up a new Missionaries of Charity House in the city of Ranchi, India. Over the next year Houses opened in Delhi, Jhansi and Agra and novices arrived from foreign countries.

As more Houses opened across India, Mother Teresa travelled to Rome to ask the Pope if he would make the order pontifical – this meant she would be allowed to open Houses across the world. In 1965, her wish was granted and the first overseas House opened in Venezuela, South America. Four years later there were five international Houses – including one in Rome. The Missionaries of Charity were truly international.

▶ No matter where they were in the world, the nuns of the Missionaries of Charity lived by the same simple rules as Mother Teresa.

Other orders

As the Missionaries of Charity grew they found they needed help with their work. An association of lay people (who do not take religious vows) was formed, as was the Missionary Brothers of Charity – an order for men who wanted to join in Mother Teresa's work but were not ordained as priests. Later, an order for women who took some holy orders but were still permitted to marry was formed, called the Lady Missionaries of Charity.

INTERNATIONAL RECOGNITION

Mother Teresa's work was valued highly in India – Nehru, the Indian Prime Minister, attended the official opening of the order's House in New Delhi in 1960.

But as time passed, news of what the Missionaries of Charity were doing began to spread across the globe too; especially when the order went international. Mother Teresa became an unlikely star.

FAME BECKONS

Mother Teresa had already had some experience of fame. In 1959, she was invited on a speaking tour of America. She felt uncomfortable with the attention, but the tour raised much-needed cash for the order's work.

She also gave interviews to magazines and television programmes, including the BBC and *Time* magazine. Her fame spread – people seemed to find something appealing in the tiny, frail-looking nun – and soon her distinctive, sari-like habit was recognisable the world over. Yet all the while she worried that the fame would distract her from her work.

◀ Although she disliked the travel, Mother Teresa spent time touring other countries to talk about her work.

The Nobel Prize

In 1979, Mother Teresa received the ultimate accolade for her work when she was awarded the Nobel Peace Prize – an annual accolade for people who have done something outstanding to promote peace and wellbeing. Over the next few years she was invited to meet two Presidents of America – Ronald Reagan and Bill Clinton. People travelled to Kolkata to visit her, too, including Princess Diana from the British Royal Family. She remained uncomfortable with the attention, but felt if it also brought money to keep the order's Houses open and helping people, then fame could be endured.

▶ Mother Teresa holding the boxes containing her Nobel Peace Prize medal and diploma.

Explosive Award

The Nobel Prize was created in 1901 by Alfred Nobel, the inventor of dynamite. There are actually six different prizes awarded every year for outstanding work in the areas of Peace, Literature, Physics, Chemistry, Medicine and Economics.

FACING CRITICISM

Mother Teresa won major international awards for her work and many people revered her as a living saint.

However, whether she sought the attention or not, there was a price to pay for her fame, and Mother Teresa faced criticism both in her lifetime, and after her death.

RUMOURS AND LIES

One common accusation levelled at her was that she used her clinics to convert Hindus and Muslims that she helped to Catholicism. There were sometimes protests outside her Houses when these rumours surfaced. However Mother Teresa always denied these allegations, stating that her order was created to help people, not convert them. Nor was there any evidence that anyone was forced to change their religion.

◀ No matter what was happening outside the gates of her Houses, Mother Teresa tried to make those inside feel safe and loved.

▶ The Houses were always crowded, and there were always people waiting to get in, too.

SUBSTANDARD CARE?

Another criticism was that the standard of care people received was well below that provided in hospitals. Critics pointed out that the nuns were poorly trained, and facilities in the Houses were not up to scratch. Supporters said that the Missionaries of Charity were set up to provide the poorest of the poor with dignity and care. The Houses were not meant to be hospitals, but to provide basic medical care for those who had nowhere else to turn.

Unwelcome

Although the Missionaries of Charity work in many countries around the world, they have not always been universally welcomed. The House which opened in Belfast in Northern Ireland closed after less than two years following reports of tensions with the local church. In 1971, the order was forced to leave the House in Sri Lanka after civil war broke out and the government told them to go. Officially this was for safety reasons but some suspected that the government didn't want the order there.

DEATH AND LEGACY

▲ Although she was old and frail, Mother Teresa continued to travel to raise the profile of her order.

As her order continued to open Houses around the world, the health of Mother Teresa began to fail.

In 1983, when on a visit to Rome to meet Pope John Paul II, Mother Teresa had a heart attack. She survived, but it was a warning that she needed to slow down – and for a woman whose whole life had been based around hard work, that was going to be a problem.

THE END

Over the next few years she was plagued by ill health. More heart problems led to three separate rounds of heart surgery. Although the operations helped, they couldn't turn back time; Mother Teresa was getting old. Finally, on 5th September 1997, Mother Teresa suffered another heart attack and died. She was 87 years old.

The news spread quickly. Outside the Mother House – the headquarters of the Missionaries of Charity in Kolkata – crowds of people arrived and stood in the pouring rain in sombre vigil for the departed nun. While this was a simple reflection of how highly Mother Teresa was regarded, the funeral showed how important she had become internationally. She was buried with full state honours – something which usually only happens for political leaders. Thousands of people lined the route her coffin took, and countries from across the globe sent representatives to her funeral.

A FLOURISHING ORDER

At the time of her death the Missionaries of Charity had outposts in over 100 countries. The order fed about 500,000 families in 1997 alone, and taught 20,000 children from the slums. Nearly 100,000 lepers received help each year, too. During a time when many orders found it hard to recruit novices, The Missionaries of Charity were expanding – it was a world away from that first slum school Mother Teresa had set up in 1948.

▼ Mother Teresa's open coffin was carried with great care and dignity by the Indian army during her funeral procession.

Missionaries of Charity Family

The order is still going strong today, with lots of different branches that together are known as the Family. Apart from Missionary Sisters, Brothers and Co-workers, there are also contemplative orders – Sisters and Brothers who devote more of their time to prayer. There are the Lay Missionaries of Charity, and two organizations for priests called the Corpus Christi Movement and the Missionaries of Charity Fathers, too.

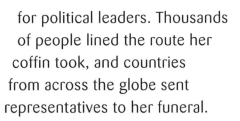

THE PATH TO SAINTHOOD

Mother Teresa and her work may still be facing criticism from some quarters, but the truth remains that she made a profound difference to the lives of many, many people.

She cared for the dying, educated the poor and tended to the needs of the sick and the forgotten. People began calling her a saint when she was still alive, but following her death there was a call for her sainthood to be made official.

HOLY WOMAN

The word saint actually means holy, and in the Catholic Church a saint is a man or a woman who is held up as an example of how to live a true Christian life. What makes a saint different from other people who live their lives in a good Christian way is that Catholics believe that a miracle can occur in the saint's name after that person has died. A miracle is something that happens without a reasonable explanation. For example, if an ill person prays to a saint and then is cured when medically they should not have got better, that would be considered a miracle.

◀ Crowds of people from around the world flocked to Rome to hear the mass to beatify Mother Teresa.

SAINTHOOD

A person cannot become a saint straight away – normally they cannot be considered for sainthood until at least five years after their death. Pope John Paul II made an exception for Mother Teresa though, and the process began after just two years. To become a saint two miracles have to occur in that person's name. The first of Mother Teresa's miracles was a woman with a tumour who was cured after praying to her; the second was a man who had a life threatening brain infection but was miraculously better overnight. Although some doctors dispute the evidence, the Vatican was happy that they were miracles. Mother Teresa became a saint on the 4th September 2016 – almost nineteen years to the day that she died!

▶ Pope John Paul II – an old man himself by that point – said a mass for Mother Teresa.

The First Saint

Before the Middle Ages, saints were chosen by the people – if a person was admired for their holiness, they were called a saint. Later, the Church made it the official process it remains today. People disagree on who the first official saint was, but it was either Saint Swibert in 804CE or Saint Udalric in 993CE.

GLOSSARY

Accolade an award

Albanians people from the country of Albania

Archbishop a high ranking post in the Catholic Church

Catholic a Christian religion with direct links to Jesus's first followers

Catechism a series of questions and answers on the Church's beliefs and teacings

Christian someone who believes in the teachings of Jesus

Compound a walled area

Destitute extremely poor

Dynamite an explosive

Embroidery using thread to decorate cloth

Hindu a believer in the god Brahman

Humility to be humble, or modest

International in more than one country

Jesuit a member of a Roman Catholic religious order, known for its missionary work

Leper a person suffering from leprosy

Leprosy an infectious disease of the skin and nervous system.

Limelight in the public view

Muslim a follower of Islam

Order an organized religious group who live in their own communities or groups

Pope the head of the Catholic Church

Terminally ill an illness that will lead to death

Tolerated put up with

Turbulent chaotic

Tumour an abnormal growth inside or outside the body

Unassuming modest

Vows promises to God

Further information

Websites

http://www.motherteresa.org/

http://www.nobelprize.org/nobel_prizes/peace/laureates/1979/teresa-facts.html

http://www.mcbrothers.org/mc_family.html

Books

Mother Teresa of Calcutta, Pascoletti, Elena, CTS 2013

Mother Teresa, Gold, Maya, Dorling Kindersley 2013

Who Was Mother Teresa?, Harrison, Nancy, Grosset and Dunlap 2015

Places to Visit

Mother Teresa's tomb, Mother House, Kolkata

INDEX